Pyrrhonic

Poems by
Stephanie L. Erdman

DOS MADRES
2017

DOS MADRES PRESS INC.
P.O.Box 294, Loveland, Ohio 45140
www.dosmadres.com editor@dosmadres.com

Dos Madres is dedicated to the belief that the small press is essential to the vitality of contemporary literature as a carrier of the new voice, as well as the older, sometimes forgotten voices of the past. And in an ever more virtual world, to the creation of fine books pleasing to the eye and hand.

Dos Madres is named in honor of Vera Murphy and Libbie Hughes, the "Dos Madres" whose contributions have made this press possible.

Dos Madres Press, Inc. is an Ohio Not For Profit Corporation and a 501 (c) (3) qualified public charity. Contributions are tax deductible.

Executive Editor: Robert J. Murphy

Illustration & Book Design: Elizabeth H. Murphy
www.illusionstudios.net

Typset in Calibri Light & Lithos Pro
ISBN 978-1-939929-83-9
Library of Congress Control Number: 2017944669

First Edition

Copyright 2017 Stephanie Erdman
All rights reserved. No part of this book may be reproduced or transmitted in any form or by any means graphic, electronic or mechanical, including photocopying, recording, taping or by any information storage or retrieval system, without the permission in writing from the publisher.
Published by Dos Madres Press, Inc.

Acknowledgements

This project owes a great debt to a lot of very dedicated and precise readers. Some of these poems, primarily "Some Kind of Meditation," borrow a lot from the experiences and stories of two dear friends: Ashley Petersen and Nathan Siery. Thank you both for supporting me and letting me share in your lives.

The erasures that appear periodically throughout the text as images are adapted and appropriated from "Woods in Spring" and "The rainbow" by Gerard Manley Hopkins and "Terribilis Est Locu Iste" and "Florentines" by Geoffrey Hill.

The fruition of this project owes a great deal to the persistent artistic commentary of Professor David Dodd Lee and he is owed deepest gratitude for his continued support and assistance.

"(excerpt from a love letter)" first appeared in *Eclectica Magazine*.

"I still live" was first published in the first issue of *Twyckenham Notes*.

For Karl and Caryl, thank you for pushing me
and giving me time to push myself.

Table of Contents

Foundation
Celebrating what I forgot — 1
Some evenings — 2
(32) — 3
I still live — 4
History in root systems — 6
The year of — 8
"Satan Without Seraphs" — 11
Paranoid — 13
Rainbow — 16
Klorofill — 17

Form
Qi gong[18] — 21
Eating the After-Birth — 22
Jeremiah 18:4 — 23
Some Kind of Meditation — 24
Third Trimester — 49
Fox Season — 50
The Title of This Poem Is A Sentence — 51

Freedom
Florentines — 55
Pyrrhonic — 56
(excerpt from an email) — 58
Between — 59
Something about margarine — 62
(excerpt from a love letter) — 64
"i thought about destroying all my work..." — 65
(excerpt from an argument) — 66
Minor Chords — 67

"Pole Turtle" or "A Statement of Class Without Words" — 68
Locus Iste — 70
Oranges — 71
Morning comes too soon for Walter Ong — 74
Driving Home in the Dark, Cheating the Speed Limit — 75
For George — 77
(excerpt from a voicemail) — 78

Notes — 81
About the Author — 95

Pyrrhonic *adj.* (ˈpɪrəʊɪk)

1. Of or pertaining to Pyrrho (360-720 b.c.e.), Greek philosopher, founder of skepticism or
2. Of or pertaining to Pyrrhonism or skepticism, Pyrrhonic doubt.
3. Those who hold the impossibility of attaining certainty of knowledge, believing that true wisdom and happiness lie in suspension of judgement.

From Denis Diderot: "Pyrrhonic or skeptical philosophy...may be reached in two possible ways which are in opposition to each other; we adopt this philosophical point of view either because we know too little, or because we know too much..."

Foundation

Celebrating What I Forgot

The sky scraping
against itself
in steel wool surging

toward making it
rain today, we
apply ourselves,

indigently, to neat
bourbons. This is how
we celebrate

the South and count
down toward the julep
months, our muddlers

in our mouths
and not speaking to one another.

I don't fold up
elegantly anymore,
expansive with age

and weariness,
cotton-tongued
at one a.m.

in the basket of your grown-up
    tricycle.

Some Evenings

while I try to scrub off my skin
the physicists theorize elegantly

into my ear. (How a cochlea
presents the Golden Ratio[1]! Nautiloid

of such aural seas.) To start
me wondering about what timeline I'm living

just 3 inches to the left. Sometimes I itch
for needles to swim the mantel of my skin, split

vulgar corpuscles. Technology inside strings sublimely
vibrates as deep inside everything. Such echoes

Gothic cathedrals were built around, buttressed.
Builders not knowing what sings

inside Geometry; just as there are words
implanted somewhere, cleft recesses of my mouth,

this gut-ache for talons to tear secrets loose.
Sometimes I try to tune this inaudible hum

of spheres with chemical bonds,
sciences of blood and want, such

adenoidal pillars—irenic, primitive.

(32)

(*Woods* ▬▬▬)

(*a*)
—the shallow folds ▬▬▬
▬▬▬ dabbled with ▬▬▬ growth,
▬▬lakes of bluebells, pieced ▬ primroses.

(*b*)
In ▬ green spots ▬▬▬
Were eyes of ▬▬▬ primrose: bluebells ▬▬
In skeins about ▬▬▬.

I STILL LIVE
For The World's Most Unfamous Artist

Born enamored
with the sea
and light

and all that
it reflects off of,
the surfaces

that were familiar
until the sunset, until
the broken glass

settled against our tongues
and the roofs of our mouths
prayer room silent.

There were ululations
over the desert
that settled into

the wombs of cactus blossoms,
small oases in the vast unforgiven.
Her name was something

like a stream that I
can't remember and she
yelled back at our echoes:

"Do not fill use yet, we are still alive."
We waited for the acerb air
to mummify us

somewhat and I remember
hearing about caves, the crystal
dormant in them

and dry, the water seeping
toward the chambers
for 10,000 years.

History in Root Systems[2]

       just below our feet, everything.
Today, I can't remember

       what I said; myth's myriad roots
breaking ground, this Babylon willow[3].
       Meagerly budded branches encircle

evening-lightened freckles of stars.
       Ignatius said, "Fortuna" once.[4]

This inheritance, this harvest (whispers).
       A drowning curl of childish
fingers; (I couldn't stop.) between

sobs—to hyperventilate, seized ceasing—
       all fireworks in breath-dark longing

just beneath fingerprint leaves. How
I couldn't stop looking.
       Inverse sphagnum moss[5]

held in the minutiae of seed
       when early-broken morning

       is how we stood, shunned from heat.
We know it's coming; gray,
       no trees here—

uncovered slumber of garden beds.
       Rake form from

these leaves, see
       coming years: ivy-kissed, full.
The moon waxes, the days are long.

    Deer steal aureate squashes,
harvest rabbits abduct our peppers.

                        Bereft tools to realize,
        dreams left to build
their nests in my eyes.

The year of

I.
realm rules; suburban
espionage and what about
problems of significance
naming the gradient of
reality awash in gray like
twilight when neighbors
light their charcoal grills.

He wonders how time passes
in other rooms more vacant
than this one. Marking time
in smoked cigarettes, bottle caps,
crushing crippling worry
needing to do, be, accomplish,
become—measuring time

that should have been enjoyed
or the theories of lives
running less than parallel.
Fall asleep in the arms of
strangers or anxiety over
what should have been said
over the decay of the moments

wondering when they'll all
come back. The realm of
broken doors and regression
and questions that seem foreign—
domestic worry or chemical
elation that's only temporary.
There's not much to expect.

II.
Realm. Rules. The
regularly scheduled
program that isn't
a mirror—I can't see
myself in. It's not the face
I don't recognize but
the names of familiar objects

strange when repeated into
the afternoon. These slants
of sunlight from those observant
windows—blind. Am I
going blind? Where
am I going? What
am I doing—should

have done—should
do? Writing. I
should be writing
becoming and transforming
things with gray names
the disapproval of pendant
lights is interruptive; just

how mother might
have done it. Judgment
inherent in being loved—
to shrink away, the
recluse playing at
what I'm pretty sure
life is come to expect.

III.
Realm rules? You
watch through spider
cracks—the cobwebbed
moments of pharmaceutical
calm. You know
the feeling of being
manufactured. Here

you are careful,
preserving the way
of things, the expectation
of return. The unsure
moments of clustered dark
and idiosyncratic plumbing,
the rattle of nascent

windowpanes or the wind
absent trees or gray
lurking things you
must name. The demands
of eyes perceived as watching,
the clatter on wood
floor in empty rooms

where time moves at some
different measure—clicks
in deep water. Sleeping,
you wonder about
the lives of things (not
quite parallel). Your
life outside expectation.

"Satan Without Seraphs"[6]

We bury carp
to bless the foundation

of our house; cook catfish
    over a fire. I try

to draw a picture of proper panfishes
in adjective while you shake your head

and narrate "Moby Dick," explaining
    why John Bonham[7] chastens

cowbells to the floor. I can't
keep meter while you paint

internal combustion in hand gestures.
The water here tastes like chlorine;

      where are the oxides
    I grew up steeped in? Smiling

villagers burnt the rood,
painted out all the storied saints.

Blankness to bombast to dull
this chapel: erased stories over vacant

walls. It's business. Buddha
    reaches under her hat

offering magic in small squares—
"Put it on your tongue." But I

mistrust science's *sativa*[8]
smell: rootless. Maybe

he'll teach his son Latin
to remember to pray, confusing

the roots of anxiety and ecstasy.[9]
Tight tremulous body all the same in sweat,

smiles. When crucifixes are just
punctured gar[10] etched in dust, seraphs

and sunfish[11] smile. We sharpen hooks
on boot heels, solder or weld

    each other, our blood
through carburetors. Buddha

whispers, "Everything is in everything
and the insides of it all are beautiful."

Paranoid

The stomachs of bricklayers
        churn
like the brass tongues

of bells about the foundations
of pillars, touched by mortar only
and fingertips. What if I'm paranoid?

What does that say
about my self-diagnosis? Perhaps
I believe my car

puts out a frequency that turns
streetlights off as I pass beneath
like the mechanical *Übermensch* of Kant's nightmares.[12]

When I first heard bluegrass,
iron oxide ran from the taps
reminding me that the Colorado River

used to be ground level; I suppose
it still is though. Strings vibrate
our perceptions, really no more special
than rubberbands or calamari.

I write myself so many notes.
Oh, the wasted miles of paper or
meters of brick and empty cans

of spray-paint! For what real purpose,
besides stroking the face of a seeming eternity
to leave a scar where once I stood, to be

a ghost of myself, paranoid and transparent,
I can still smell the essences of spiders
in the cloying dark, it presses in deep

whispers where the walls have been: a clutch
of *phronima*[13] crawling over the Wreckage,
for the citrus taste in the buttresses

of my own cathedral. Empty and cobwebbed mostly
twisted in. Practicing my lightsaber moves
and blues guitar to forget my neighbor's

reverse agoraphobia—she won't leave me alone—
like erosion sloughing the great crag
of Abraham Lincoln's nose into
a more precise point. "There is no need
to worry, for everything there is a season."[14]
Turn, turn, turn. The needle is broken

on the turntable, another $60 we don't have
so we can dance to Stevie Ray Vaughan again,
to recall the evening we spent indoors and, enamored

with dinner, glowing in wine; you look at me
like something, a pink primrose, when I feel only
soapweed[15] unspectacular waiting. I will sip my wine.

I will watch the *Perseids* burn away the stars
(or was it the *Leonids*?) Ave Maria, gracia plena...
Our Father full of grace... I begin strong

every time like Sisyphus only to forget
those childhood songs but no one is listening
for Christ's sake. We are all lost and by His grace
we are found unable to eat breakfast
    because of ulcers ten years old.

██ rainbow

                See ██████,°
He drops his ██ roots in ████████,
And ████████ dispenses green;
████ his other foot ██ miles beyond
He rises from ██████ villages
That bead ████; did ever Havering ████
Breathe in such ███? or the ████ elms
  { ████████ slight their distanced green?
  { Slight with ███ violet their ██████ green?

or

Mask'd ██████ violet disallow their green?

Klorofill

There is no exploit left
where dreams melt in early-morning
television; anonymity of veins. Fear

to try or not (when
arms encircling are sometimes just
the crescent moon.) I am

paint-splattered, a rusted lightning rod
in extreme, always lost &
herring-boned with flashing streetlights after

4 a.m. Monochromatic. Decisions wander &
call "sanctuary" amid fruit flies.
(I have scrubbed the poetry

out of my hands—my
bones are filled with smoke
from cartons of indifferent cigarettes.)

I hide my splinters from
you—deep in my skin
& afraid of the pain

of absence. Removal? Preferring to
let them root deep in
my bones. Regenerating fingers to

feed off my blood, as
I do, making room for
itself, an invasion like music.

Burning the mosaic of books
I've collected for instant need
of water. I am always

thirsty now. Gallons of water
to cool the summer in
my organs, to soften the

soil around my toes. My
skin like birch paper &
leaves palm up in breezes

before the rain, windows in
words between where carpets feign
    photosynthesis in daylight.

Form

QI GONG[16]

Your house is reclaimed by trees—
    the world is not as you would make it,
as your house is reclaimed by trees;

the world is not as you would make it,
    road roiling by & you don't believe in midwinter.
A world not as you would make it.

Road roiling by & you don't believe in midwinter,
    when the impulses of youth were no tragedy;
road rolling by & you don't believe

in impulses or tragedies
    the green glow like beneath the sea
of impulses or tragedies.

The green glow like beneath the sea
    light always burning in the vine-covered windows
a green glow like beneath the sea.

Lights always burning in vine-covered windows
    all sand where the hills were
the light's always burning;

that sand where the hills were
    tattered leaves & lost shingles,
slippered sand where the hills were.

Tattered leaves & lost shingles
    & your house is reclaimed by trees
under tattered leaves & lost shingles
    your house is reclaimed by trees.

Eating the After-Birth

Awake in the world's feedlot,
(we're eating the after-birth)—
Panes of windows cold to
touch. Sunday dialogue of lazy.

"We're eating the after-birth."
Locked in gray noise neon
touch—Sunday dialogue of lazy
TV, papercuts from the Business Section:

locked in gray noise. Neon,
things aren't better yet. "Groceries."
TV, papercuts from the Business Section—
"...are getting expensive, have gotten..."

(Things aren't better yet.) "Groceries?"
"Utilities—" (Winter has gotten cheap.)
"—are getting expensive, have gotten..."
Remnants of cornstalks, iced potholes—

Utility: winter has gotten cheap
panes of windows cold too &
remnants of cornstalks, iced potholes
awake in the world's feedlot.

JEREMIAH 18:4[19]
After the death of Muhammad Ali

There was a man glowing
like a house upon the hill.
We took pictures of him only
when he bled, clenched hands raised

like a house upon the hill;
we spoke his name
when he bled, clenched hands raised.
The lights all on until they weren't.

We spoke his name,
"you are the most important."
The lights all on until they weren't
to build a realm extending to—

"you are the most important" and
limited by—the horizons,
a built realm extending to
as far as you can see.

SOME KIND OF MEDITATION[18]

"You could not have wished to be born at a better time than this, when everything has been lost."
                                        Simone Weil[19]

I.
An impulsive tongue, brain licked by curses. Prose,
signal flag, "Diver Down." Billboard voices in praise
such hymns above blank windows & weed growth
more than sidewalk. Heels clatter uneven & beer close
enough to being right. Speech (the slavering flows,
reason with a mad dog—) windows of houses, those

white-blank eyes, don't hint what those
inhabitants see looking out. We talk in prose
philosophically, & nebulae (these ebbs & flows)
all beyond our heads. How naming is just like praise!
We three seek approval in side-glances, how close
we are to gone from here. We know the undergrowth

of words after acid at 3 a.m. Methods to measure growth
in sheets of paper or birch skin. Empty bottles; those
beers went first. Marvel-blue smoke, suburban close
& how lonely rural seems in the wake of industry. "Prose
is dying like Pittsburgh," you say. "Paths that praise
the Monongahela almost burning like the oil flows

of the Susquehanna." I nod. You know where poison flows
now. Somewhere you have collected the growth
charts of a black & white bean. Living in slow praise
of patience, planning. Brevity asleep those
months still, A#10 envelopes of folded prose
& insomnia. Hold those letters close

still. Our voices try to remind you, how close
you couldn't see her. A word that flows
past your ears unnoticed. I want to build prose
from questions, to pretend no jealousy in growth,
to fill my mouth with hops—teeth clamping those
ramblings shut. I want my hands to speak in tongues, praise

the known world. Echoes only praise
themselves, empty mouths. Bound pages close
at hand like deadlines, snow-blank. Those
times we could say "No" & didn't. Time flows
slower in hindsight, minds deep in ivy growth.
We share a scholar's dementia in epitaph prose.

II.
Empty shoes along the stairs, individual skins, a tale
implied over tile floors. Psalms lack detail,
bare praise on onion skin while Solomon's song regale
the shape of breasts piously. Truck-stop magazine err
egregiously in such fluorescent light. To borrow choral
tongues to immortalize concrete underpasses stale

with the press of people who clutch at stale
wafers dipped in wine & held for the dying. Whose tale
has more music? Echoed rumbles of forgotten stomachs' choral
cries (more than six & larger). An afterthought, lost detail
we three deep in cities like rivers. Old World Wanderers, err
like rivers, feeling cut from sails—winds regale

lost coasts we've forgotten names for, winds regale
faces we've built in words. In early morning, breaths stale,
the sky lightening—we list our mistakes. Clumsy tongues err
& we breathe out clouds. What are we? A tale
to be whispered across continents soon, denying details,
we pretend & revel—shared words choral.

Pretend my verses will always reach. Open mouths, coral
adorations but only gawping. I will always send words, regale
absent ears, find the perfect hyphenation, confound detail.
Everything feels heavy now, balance my stalled
tongued & rusted pens; I wish for some tale
to overtake me, cradled between ego & air.

Your braids sway, "There's too much space in the air,"
move to light candles behind stained glass. Mute or choral,
such story cycles under your hat, there are Greeks, a tale
10 years lost at sea when we too cry out for fame—regale
Sirens 'til they sleep on outcroppings of stolen
fish heads & rotted spines. Show me all the detail

in rice vinegar & bean curd. What fanatical details
we find in the Apocalypses & fingerprints err
toward being record grooves. We are air inside walls: stale,
secret. Chords built of the breaths in all the choral
trains across the cold river. Liquor-warm we watch, regale
the crowd, write us into The Escapist's tale.

III.
Sound scourges my head but, like Beethoven, I compose
with deaf fingers reproducing a shade that goes
behind the sound. Like a raven, notch my tongue[20] & expose
the words to light in the croaking pages. Lay prone
or supine in abbreviated daylight, thought slows
somnambulant. I've lost the music to my prose;

possessing only one mode (anxious as the ego in prose)
I build cocoons in insulated wires, diagrams compose
the rules of resistors. Always awake; my brain never slows
churned panic or eyelids or words. Night goes,
day goes, I don't remember the calculus of time. Prone
& motionless, the mattress molds me, nerves expose

the biting surfaces haloing my tongue, expose
inverted pockets, shrug. Not well-versed in the prose
of asking forgiveness or any other iniquity. Just as prone
to vulgarity as "sir" or "ma'am." Common, we all compose
identity like Windsor knots;[21] careful choose what goes
over us. Recidivist conscience never slows

this anxious churning behind my eyes. My tongue slows,
licking the flavor from each word to paste to paper, expose
its lacey intoxication, translucent, just as skin goes
through lingerie like meaning. I meant this as prose;
a Statement of Purpose or supplication—to compose
prayers between hymns—anything to sleep again, prone

& sweating, tangled. To wake or sleep, accident-prone
& gray. Unsureness in the tiled halls. Time slows.
There's a nocturne here, awake, tempos compose
notes, harmonize between dissonance—to expose
the gritty ligaments that stitch the world. No prose
left in my auger tongue, no logic, my sentence goes

on forever. I don't punctuate with care & syntax goes
in favor of artfulness—a low form of deceit. Prone
to ego & ear, fall in favor of all the better prose
that I imagine to exist. Either my pen or possessor slows,
I'm not sure what I pay for in coordination & expose
my two-ply cardboard self to retire or de-compose.

IV.

We three, some morning, wait for Olson's exhale
& break his syntax across our knees: smaller, musical
bytes. Against the sharp-edged way the self-flagellates inhale
& bleed down their bare backs. Can the wretched prevail
against this modern plague? Open mouths outweigh & keel
gap-toothed words to sea beds. Like from the eyes of Saul, scale

slough my tongue, a mermaid disease, & yet we scale
the shores to lose our tales. Burst cloudward, exhale
some Atlantean language, long-dead barnacles, our keel.
Images slap our tongues, small fishes, the water musical
only to Handel. Ebb or neap no matter, the tides prevail
or the moon, sand scatters & castles collapse, yawp, inhale.

Sirens sing still. Wax-stopped, watch Odysseus inhale
& strain & gasp. Lungs & ship sides rimed in scale
still brave straits. 10 years lost at sea, for fame, prevail
& keep the songs of Kings. Music & magic exhale
a common root in Greek,[22] we begrudge their musical
mysticism & write talismans to name each spine a keel.

Red sky at morning, we pray at compass points, bless our keels
against the curse over the Intracoastal, its salt inhale
burns our throats to the epiglottis. Primate bladders, musical
& burning over the water. Running the texture of its salt scales
along our mutable lips, cracked to bleed. Exhale
pink foam, mad dogs at sunrise. Words prevail

we hide lists in our gapped shoe soles. Words prevail
in us when our syntax atrophies. Cranial sutures keel
to each skull, eyes level & regulated. We exhale
to condensate glass for secret messages, sharply inhale
to hide them away. Vestiges of mettle on walls, scale—
water never forgets. In chlorine or salt-water, musical

ringing down drains, gurgling deep as stomachs. Musical
digestions. We right ourselves in sewage & cess, prevail
against tides & regulations, telling time on the scale
of the million-mile distant moon. Equator keel
against our blue-green axis. Oceans or cave maws inhale
just as we three might. Our eons: a single, solar exhale.

V.

You don't pray for sleep anymore but Ambien subverts review
to slide you, feet first, into blackness. Pursue
the preceding calm when the anxiety sleeps away its truth
when you can ignore the green voice biting through
your mind's brief meningeal comfort. What is it the pills do
for you that you are less afraid of the Other? How

Hyde you seem to yourself late at night & chain-smoking, how
you have no stomach for real food or comfort but review
the labels of empty bottles nightly. It's just balancing you do
now, a mortgage against your woken faculties, you pursue
hourly unknowing—a blankness whispered in neurons through
gray daylight too. Talismans, music, objects hold some truth

still & you cling to those. Look for proof, eternal truth
is all you'll accept. You've lost count in cartons, how
cigarettes & orange juice share units & you see through
that trick. Your head is owned by inventories, you review
numbers constantly. "Readiness!" That War ideal—pursue
some pre-suburban persona. Shave clean like soldiers do

& surround yourself with trenches. Bare-boned feet do
boots no justice & you shed them, wood-footed. What truth
can stop a higher calling? Arm yourself & pursue
invading bats—such omens—banish blackness out. How
homesteads crumbled into the Dust Bowl (not so!). You review
your defenses, seal perimeters, stand stark sentry through.

that prescribed blankness. Write your orange lists through
the hours when the cul de sac doesn't stir. Alone, you do
some penance that scars your throat, review
your over-grown reflection. Mercury is the only truth.
Wanting prophesy, you get only a mirror image. How
nothing is quite real when the pills take hold & pursue

you into ignorant rest—what time is there? Pursue
each geometric facet of lost time, storm the gates through
midnight & put marks on the moon's face. This is how
we evolved obstinate & without clever feet. You do
you own surgery: whittle away your heavy doors against truth
and face East anointed gold. A final, cold review.

VI.
Impulsive tongue, possessing words & eating fiction,
waking each morning: an empty gut & toothed revision
of self. We touch the hems of the Virgin of Fatima,[23] her reaction
to war: baking blackbirds for the Pope, paid devotion
in hidden catacombs. Her secrets. Bought absolution
in Mediccis' bloody gold. Bones held still, an encryption

of relics. Revealed to successors like Newman's[24] encryption
of line or landscape. We assign value to fiction:
a scale of "white lie" to faith healer. A bead-strung absolution
made in power lines & farmland? Flood waters recede—a revision—
the land seen again. Land rising up, each creature's devotion
to the primordial wet with reticent gills. Legs a reaction

to mud creeping beneath our scales, thunderousness a reaction
to plenty. We line our pockets with fossils—encryption
of our ticking mortality. Wear our lovers' scapular devotion
in bared metal on skin. Shame, too, is an act of fiction
hermetic erasures felt like lips. Each saint's fob is a revision
of what we mean by "love." Opening artifacts to absolution.

We remember brewing blood to drink our enemies' absolution,
thieving warrior spirits to sleep in the dark without fear, a reaction
to firelit shadows. Talismans safe between breasts, revision—
an effort against progress. A dance of genetic encryption
toward the meaning of "be." Fables & gods for all things, fiction
fighting science way. The difference between need & devotion.

We still call down saints in secret, a test of their devotion
to saintliness. Clean hands clasped & bleeding for absolution
not this world but the next. Not every stigmata built of fiction
or piety (maybe nettlecloth). Friars blister silent reactions,
cut by trod thorns. Squinting over Latin encryption
& hunched in gloaming. They copy each vellum revision

blessed by gamboling margins. One slipped revision,
the Wicked Bible[25] must be burnt. Self-denial for devotion:
mortifying the flesh, ash-lined gut, & encryption
of Christ's own pain. Symbols of minute absolution
is all we ask of Our Lady, prophesy our fates. This reaction
to the death we deal—small-handed three—naïve fiction.

VII.
Your grandfather gave you a camera eye. Skilled depiction
of a world pressed in glass & shutter. Smooth friction
lens baffle. You fold your fingers & cradle the sun left in
the aperture, how it paints faces on paper or finds dejection
in trash flotsam. In the gloaming, you catch an ion
like a firefly buried in subatomic particles. All the fiction

of tiny orbits, exchange of electrons ring false like fiction
at the roots of your hair held tight. Each layer of depiction
is a new sweater you wrap yourself in. Building static an ion
at a time. Everything you gather together held in friction
like curled toes. When scraps of paper teach you dejection,
you gather them together—biblical stones or tongues—left in

meditation for a moment, forgetting what Tartarus left in
the Hundred-Handed.[26] We sit around you, worry about fiction
we don't know. How much of life is illusory? Dejection
that waits behind doors. Every hungry ghost is a depiction—
us without skin, a face you recognize. You knew. Friction
from tucking your hat in at the corners. A gathering of ion

clusters at your temples poise to discharge. Place an ion
in every beggar's cup—a gift of power. Look for what's left in
them; husks in coats like flower petals. No fiction.
You're scared of the thing inside you that wells up with fiction
trusting what the camera shows you: light & pure depiction.
You can pile it in boxes, hold the truth, mask dejection

from the recesses of your room, collect shadows from dejection,
from moonlight coming in. No curtains. A gap enough for an ion
to slip into your bed. Trace lines on carpet, depiction
of the dance of days. You take pictures of footprints left in
carpet & file away the pictures just naming fiction
when you see it. What is there between people? Friction

between two hands. Heat-bloomed palms in cold, no friction,
though everything touches everything still space for dejection.
How there's space everywhere & smooth surfaces are fiction
but photos aren't; your grandfather gave them to you. An ion
loose in the sea. Your pictures, remade in words, left in
some unvisited room until you release them on paper: depiction.

VIII.
Plague flies in, or Pestilence, lost & we don't pray enough
we disobey or take pride. We read Job. His maladies imbue
us with a capricious God & we are pawns He drew
into being. So we collect our talismans to hang in doorways to
keep the words out. They fall dead around ears, rain's tattoo
on car roofs. Music in clouds overhead, we count it in three-

four time. What maps in our futures? Scattered, we three,
words in winding sheets. St. Paul, to the Ephesians, is enough
to thrall the flung tribes of nomads. Dot matrix tattoos,
expanding nets,[27] Egyptians blessed pregnant women to imbue
their wombs with stars. Dancing priestesses stripped down to
become common mothers. 12,000 years since heavy rains drew

sand across the plateau—only magic in the desert. We drew
our lots & split the rags like spoils; we keep relics in three
piles. How many bones did saints have? St. John's tooth to
bless the just-born on their baptismal crowns, no magic enough
to grow them any better. Stale wafers & bruised knees imbue
us with Famine in our mouths, strike the face of tile. A tattoo

like the Highland drums or ragged breathing. A tattoo,
the Spear of Destiny,[28] we put power in our mouths. Sigils drew
out blessing from skin & scab. We seek symbols to imbue
with prophesies, what War buried at Fatima. Three
shadows, long in mourning, the curtain ripped open just enough
to show the people the tabernacle a last time, the rain fell to

quench raving mouths or quell tears. We carry splinters to
Constantinople, the True Cross rises over the rivers. Tattoo
some name to yourself that only you can see, secret enough
to make you human. Old rivers, Tigris & Euphrates, drew
the world to themselves & built ziggurats over Death. Three
centuries made a young garden until the serpent came to imbue

the fruits with bitter worms, a medicine was needed. To imbue
Man with knowledge of his place. Adam blindly giving names to
what he couldn't possess, Eve, a woman without pain. We three
believe in rediscovery, our peach is wearing thin & we tattoo
"apple" over our voice boxes. Range the desert, draw
seekers to ourselves like pilgrims to Mecca. Are words enough?

IX.

Impulsive tongue, licking wounds while I sleep; poetry
in the dark like Braille. In form, there is artistry
I suppose. Or joinery, fitting everything together in carpentry
dovetails & logic. To be a technician, to knock & gain entry
to the world. To tie it up like a gift & perform ministry
stripping souls out. I'm afraid to think this way, mostly,

I make no sense of lack empathy. Magic is over my head, mostly
in devotional painted ceilings. Sometimes, I wonder about poetry
whether it's art or utility or synapses misfiring ministry
to some lost cerebral process, skull-clad, secret artistry
protected like cataphracts[29] in battle, denying entry
to whatever great cities hid. Blessed St. Joseph's carpentry

knitting God into the realm of Man. Those who practice carpentry
still pray to him like looking at Schuyler raptured mostly
maybe stealing. I build a house of books, wait outside for entry
to this land of pages, the weight of my voice within poetry.
Someone told me to sharpen my teeth at the edges of artistry—
determination, the hard-scrabble choice. Or ministry.

Can I just allay myself of words, travel deep for ministry?
Only saints wear nettlecloth. To fit words together, carpentry
of syntax or balance, the acrobatic within artistry:
construct everything to impress. An old sweater, I am mostly
unassuming. I feel my mouth open too often & hide poetry
in boxes & bales. The saints burrow under my tongue, beg entry

to my prayers & I swear against them. My fingers are entry
to such words. I scratch my way in, sew my own shroud. Ministry
of plague doctors to chase miasmas. The Rites[30] are poetry,
too, the last they'll hear above the dirt & pine box carpentry
if they're lucky enough to not get ditched. Lost bones mostly,
sinners not anticipating the Enlightenment, rebirth of artistry

with praise. New hymns & painted Hells. Shared root of artistry
& artifice—gradient flattery like every Psalm is an entry
in a log of hyperbole. I sit paranoid in caves & mostly
unworthy. (There is no self in myself anymore.) No ministry
upon Jerusalem, the Psalmist just a man. Kingdom of carpentry
in adobe huts. Not a messianic heritage but mud-cast poetry.

X.
You twisted your fingers in his hair that night, addictive
the way the light was just above the carpet. It
seemed like your hands were moving forever ago. Impulsive
fingers, forever touching the soft surfaces of things: this
is how you remember. Tattoo textures into fingerprints, if
you puzzle-piece it all together. The way the world needed Eve

to make us wise. Knowing is what you regret the most, even
the eyes of strangers glow sickly. Your eyes too—addictive
search for a torture kit in the basement. Attic of the body, if
the ladder folds, he couldn't get back in these wide windows. It
boils your prayers like fever that beds you on the carpet. This
space you're running out of. Verses in the DSM-IV31, impulsive

need to memorize the gospel. To spit it out. The impulsive
dosage in your pocket thinks you'll be well again & eaves
running over in the evening spell out music. Just this
quiet in the gloaming—is alone what makes you ill? Addictive
personalities cloying the candy-wax hallways & it
seems echoes outlive the patients. Fifteen questions, if

you knew the right answers, they wouldn't ask; if
you weren't sick inside your skin you would know. Impulsive
questioning drowns out the car radio, dims the streetlights. It
is Lilith32 & her bird feet on the sill! You marvel at her even-
numbered ribs, her demon children & owl nests. The addictive
lull of your Red Sea lovers, you turn your hands like this:

palms out, an Old Testament prayer behind this
curtain of hat-bound hair. Freedom waits on the wrong side if
you jump the railing. Push out your chest. Aseptic, addictive.
Wonder if you'll every paint anything placid. Impulsive,
categorize those diseased minds when it was only devils. Eve
was cast out by three angels because she couldn't fly; it

makes no difference in the sting, the coccyx scorpions wear. It
drips a serum onto your eyelids so you can sleep & this
is just a dream of flying. There are no pills for this uneven
sense of self. You know the names of words that worry lives in, if
you call them, they'll exorcise. They have batwings, impulsive
whispers. You know looking for your own sickness is addictive.

XI.

She's still there when you drink too much. "There's a hierarchy
in the system." You already know. A sponge cake density
in the words playing inside your head. You know geometry
is different with naked women & you're pretty sure "idolatry"
is a sleeping pill or some other deadly sin. Beer lacks potency
& pharmacology fails your foresight. There's poetry

in the wings of bats along the ceiling & you write poetry
in spilled salt. You preserve a language preserving hierarchy
& those great social injustices. Losing whatever potency
was in saying "I'm not that kind of guy." Suburban density
& echoes across the frozen grass. You taught her idolatry
& tried to show her the vastness of the sky, the geometry

of common shapes to constellations by other names. Geometry
that came from cradle of civilizations, carried. The poetry
of naming (not "What will we name it?") the latent idolatry
of procreation. You've taken too much. "There is a hierarchy
in the system." We all know. Measuring the density
of our own drunk tongues. We marvel at stars & the potency

of beer. "What do you wonder all alone?" The potency
of having to ask again. You write about what geometry
resides in Iesus Nazarenus Rex Iudaeorum,[33] how the density
of Osmium speaks of Ozymandias. The words that drip poetry
into your glass, forensic odontology edging pints. "Heirarchy
is in the system still?" Just ridges & proteins split idolatry

from conviction. The empty rooms you preserve in idolatry
too. & you unpack furniture, room to room, hamster potency
inside this habitrail. When she whispered "hierarchy"
into you as you slept, sated. Benjamin's[34] abstract geometry
that played on your unsuspecting eyelids. Write poetry
to push bats back, ward off this curse of threes. Density

in the inert self; you don't remember resting. The density
in the nighttime air between your lips, practice idolatry,
pray to the after-images burned into your bed. Write poetry
& exorcise the demons out, you know their names. Potency
knows what can happen when it has already. Organic geometry
when you drink too much & crumple, crushed by hierarchy.

XII.
We three look out windows on the evening, passive,
in wait for the words we need said. Wound in wind. The stiff
limbs of what we were extend across seas between us, deceive
the distance. Everything rushes in to fill this collapse with
roaring tides. Tentative feet walk across the sound, language is
just a fishing boat we throw rocks at. Mix up clay with spit

daub the eyes of birds so their songs can see. Spit
in the ear-pits of desert vipers to hide in the sand, a passive
heat signature. Rocks are not always about food as bread is.
We three shadows in the desert, serpent-voices aside, stiff
& steel-toed. We still feel purpose & shake our heads with
derision. Krishna draws maidens to his tree branch, deceived

in their nakedness, into mirage & blistered feet. Deceivers,
we kick stars into the sky, swear blood oaths to scorpions, spit
words at each other across blistered dark that grows cold with
waning sand. Vagaries, dunes, littered landscape & the passive
world beneath the starred domes of our skulls. My tongue stiff
& salt-coated, the words leeching out familiar moisture. Is

this where we're to be buried? Sea anemones; no water is
their Saharan legacy.35 Stare into our pitted lungs, deceive
the shimmering air as clouds, high-hung & merengue-stiff.
We three shadows 'til there is only sun, left with manna spit
from the dregs of heaven. We blink and wait, passive
wish fulfillment, we talk of "someday" & resign ourselves with

woolen sighs. We wake up & wash our hair with
our dead in the orange-peel sun, find out the message is
hidden tea leaves in the corners of our eyes. Passive
& crepuscular, we amble in the doe-tailed dark & deceive
the glass out of sand. Cat-footed, we dance & sing the spit-
curl out of the sea. "Will you play at being rip-tied & stiff

with fiction?" No need to nod collectively, spilled salt stiff
in our hair; we remember being lizards & fish before, with
tails bought in the protean ocean, gift shop of genetic spit
& shine. To have dropped the gilling is miraculous, is
bipedal with hope. Love in the language of drowning, to deceive
in coarse flailing yet, somehow, entrap hearts still mutely passive.

XIII.

This impulsive tongue's tale, late-night
prose, palimpsest devotion. Through sea-salted
poetry or piss-poor fiction—a voice,

passive still. Emergent exhale, soft-palate
prose & paint knives enough to cut
poetry out. We worship fiction, deified still…

Third Trimester

Coughing up benign tissue that could have been or would be in another world. Somehow this all feels too familiar, that's the part that's saddest. I ignore these symptoms, stretching against the muscle spasms. (Maybe this year Spring will never come...) Somewhere I heard this is the season of capricious woman; something about the Sky never quite showing her hand. The drifts are deep outside my windows and I'm so sick of chipping ice off the porch just to get the bills out of the mailbox. The maple tree out front hasn't begun its annual precocious budding. (Maybe this is the year that Spring won't come again.) The anxiety feels familiar, something I've carried with me from childhood. It's almost comforting to be visited by the same yearly worries, irrational as they may be. I want to write about the worry but think about rolling the clots between my fingertips instead.

    Sleeping Snow, I wonder
        about what secret names she
            called me before I was born.

Fox Season
for Thomas

I realize late there's a man somewhere behind these words and you startle me. "I chewed open a woman for lunch." Something shudders like Spring out of her bivalve slush and I don't know that the aortic quivering is actually mine (I lay no claim to it). How to catalog this shiver? What is its Latin, etymologic love? I think I would call you that name to unzip your skin a bit, to know you when you're unsteady. There are pictures of you only I would know to take and you might look something like me in your zebra skin; we could lay our scars over each other's and you might laugh at their shadows, I think. There's a naked Poseidon swimming in your vodka tonight but he's so benevolent you drink him down like tonic.

    Wanting me to send
        cigarettes by mail or with
            a specter of Spring herself.

The Title of This Poem Is A Sentence

Are you still escaping? Splitting silk with your sharpened knee,
the baritone rumble on your tongue. She comes to you
cocooned in just a raincoat—an old trope in heels—and there's
work to do, unfurling locomotion in pumped blood. Like
you could plant words in some <u>place</u>, perpetually lit, to flit
away and search out variegated nectars with that learned grace
in your fiddlehead proboscis.

   Capture tongue in glass
   mounted on a pin
       to take inside with you, kept
       and dusted, preserved and dead.
           What colors you had
              to command. Still & lost—

Freedom

FLORENTINES

Horses, black-lidded mouths ▮
▮ white: well-groomed ▮ warriors ▮,
▮ feuds forgotten, ▮ forgotten
▮ cavalcade passing, ▮ not far-off;
▮ faces damnable and serene.

Pyrrhonic

> "Should they succeed in convincing us that the instrument nature gave us stands in no relation to the weight we have to move, what conclusion could we draw from this?"
>
> -Denis Diderot[36]

Today, I am going
to drink all
this coffee and
live forever

in a perpetual state
of buzzing
in the vast

superdark—the
space living
in everything—the
moments

in
which words are
haloed
black holes

on battled edges
colliding bodies
(black binding

light around itself)
gravitational pull
of dense absence
plagiarism inherent

in the caffeinated
and collapsing or
recurring masticated

thoughts trying
to make sense
of aggrandizement
on

scale of the cosmos
when my fingers
are coated
with
a wet sand:
inferior grounds.
The acid burn
in

my stomach
tells me I can't
I am...
Going to drink

all
    this coffee.

I wanted to say something about pomegranates before the juice had dried on my fingers, fighting the urge to draw the portrait of a man with a six-cylinder engine where his clock-work heart could be; how all I want to do today is sit here in my pajamas and eat pomegranates while my green tea cools; how pomegranates are more winter in my mind than snow (oh if they'd fall from the laden clouds instead!); how the prescient Greeks knew this about me before I was born and put the name Persephone on my tongue; how naïve to trust the intentions of a fruit so reticent to spill its guts from mottled and capricious gills; there's a trick to cleaning them (you know this already) the pips sink away from the floating rinds in a bowl of hot water and I rake out the remnants with arthritic fingers; how I'm fighting the charcoal stains on my lips and wash them clean in grenadine.

(excerpt from an email)
December 2015

Between

i. Proteins

Whisper into alleys
burning by, obsessed
    with reverberations

Of the subtle space between
clasped hands; prayer between
    cells between molecules between

Atoms between particles between
caverns of vibrating
    mitochondria—A kiss

Is a shortening
of space; an embrace
    the compression of space

Encapsulates two beings
full of spaces, like fishnets
    or lace, holes tied together

By proteins:
A-G-T-G-T-A-C-C-A-G-T-C-G-T-A-C-C[37]
    twisted like ropes

Around the space. Substitutions
to make us less
    chimp. Individual—

II. Perception

red cells; the first
    true travelers of distance.
you are a galaxy

unto yourself—oblique
    organs are haloed planets. blood
rushes from

the lungs to fill with air
    when every noise
uttered between lips

is only audible
    because the song
shakes the space between

molecules of air:
    oxygen, carbon dioxide, carbon monoxide
some of the breathable poisons.

vibrating waves
    toward the aural shores,
the leafing of atomic trees

over the desert to bend
    the grasses of the inner ear
to push the substance and space against—

III. Interpretation

    The eardrum, small bones:
Malleus, incus, stapes;
To churn the ocean

    Of the cochlea across
The cochlear nerve for the brain
To misinterpret, the kiss

A slap, flattening
The sub-particles of space
Against a cheek, brown eyes.

    The embrace is
A thrown handkerchief
That was never really touched

    (like nothing is touched). The spiral
Arms of the circulatory system
Continue to roil around

    The gravity of organs
Indirectly fed. Travelers collide,
Frictionless. Never touch.

    These whispered alleys move
Space to erode thin
Tissues of brick walls.

SOMETHING ABOUT MARGARINE[38]

Tying our hands in advance,
cupped around cathedrals
of pause. Speaking of
value—or judgment—

Of light where engorged
seas lapped breakwater over
our breakfast table, broken yolks.
Monks with pumice-rounded[39]

skulls—in the dark, pondering
light—wrote Kyries[40] without
the octave (sharp pictographs
relating tones to one another).

Four-line staff of jacklighting
deer or spotlighting carp
with spears. Gripping
giant, muscled heads

like the torsos of philand'rous
lovers. Damned ugly with
their wet bellies. Some Proteus![41]
    "the sailor in his boat

        balances equally against
        the infinite forces
        of the ocean. (Remember
        that a boat is a lever.)"

Remember how breath is toned
    coffee-coated chords—
the music of tide pools,
mollusks, barnacles;

those words we don't say
to one another. We
yell across the lunging
sound. We're made of

harbors—how concrete sets
underwater: mechanics lost
for ages.[42] Dampen fingers before
they touch. Barbed wire blank—

> "At every moment the helmsman—
> by the weak, but directed, power
> of his muscles on tiller and oar—
> maintains equilibrium with air and water."

The untranslated notes we leave.
I remember when we still
pretended at subtle calculus
when phone lines draped too deeply

apart. Distance and dinner
burned when we imprinted
each other with couch pleats
    ignorant of all those equations...

> "There is nothing more beautiful
> than a boat."

There was something I wanted to tell you, something on
my tongue like ghost peppers and nutmeg; I wanted to ask you
where all the deer went in hunting season, whether they can
see all the safety orange and know to stay off the roads; I
wanted to ask you if you can feel how we're all pierced by
starlight and how there are miles of asphalt run under
our palms as we grow older; there was something
important that I meant to write down, some perfect words
that were like an incantation for beauty, that I wanted to roll
around in my mouth for a while and share with you, I wanted
to make music with you but my fingers are blunt and stubborn
(I broke the middle one, you remember? It looks like a lightning
rod now, like the tip is on sideways, like oak trees look in winter
when they're naked, remember?) I meant to write something
for you, a slip of paper with the password so I'd recognize you
when you come home and my mind is fuzzy from being
elsewhere (not that I stop know <u>you</u> when I go, I am just
less <u>me</u> every time I come back, you see) I meant to leave
this chair today, I meant to do something important but I forgot
what the word was; I wanted to tell you about how it's only
wonderful when <u>you</u> drive me places, how I wouldn't trust
anyone else quite as completely in my shitty car (even though
you talk with your hands when you're excited and we stagger
between lanes and laugh when we're silent, remember?);
I wanted to remember how the sky seems to pool in blue holes[43]
over the flat places in Michigan like it remembers at night how
hay fields look stubbled in lopseed[44] each summer.

(excerpt from a love letter)
2/15/2015

"I THOUGHT ABOUT DESTROYING ALL MY WORK..."[45]
(after cliff weber)

*i haven't talked to my father in over a year
    -answering machines don't count for even ½

*when i was still small enough to curl into the rear footwell
he would push the v8 in his Crown Victoria and race the airplanes
 as they departed Indianapolis
    -if he had won
     would i be in this blank room while this woman
     buttered in dark skin
     tries to convince me i'm an addict?

You told me once my smile was like snagging salmon, slick and off-putting, so I stopped. I stopped singing because you told me that I sounded raw, my syllables too vegan. I step sideways around our bed sheet barriers and carefully pick my hair out of your dinner, stay up late erasing my shadows. If I prayed it would be just becoming a pillar of salt. I roll your sleeping pills between my calloused fingertips and wait. Dampened paroxysms and clamped teeth to not interject your dreams.

At night, I imagine the sun on corpseflowers and gullwings; in the day, I wait for the moon in the beaks of gar (they are the vicious river). I run deep in the muck-dug river, the flotsam medical waste and paper pulp bleach. I want to rest with fish rot on the lilypads, a tail only a freshwater mermaid would have—like a steelhead's or a cottonmouth. In the humid morning, my head is wreathed with cottonwood silk, my cheeks are red like windburn and one of my eyelids droops. The more I look like my mother, the less you watch my mouth waiting to interrupt my droning words.

(excerpt from an argument)
July 2014

Minor Chords
For Jay Bailey

memory
things lost:
keys, pens, the promise
of moonlight over farmland

like writing in cursive,
not knowing what comes next
until the last second
where fingers follow

strings that slide loose
like an unused loom.
melancholy man,
trapped inside his music

but afraid of the power
dormant in his piano
of lost keys, minor chords
knowing only unimportant

answers and almost believing
the old stories you tell
about your youth over drinks
when there is fiction

filling your mouth, the moon,
high over farmland, peculiar
in its soft light until
you think about stars

dwindling
reaching this span
of sky millions of years
too late.

"Pole Turtle" or
"A Statement of Class Without Words" [46]

You fey child, fleshly
history of fulgurites[47] held
between your thighs (as

though holding somehow made
him yours.) Eyes blind
by faculae;[48] you whisper

"Flambeaux," blessed by their
French name. Whisper back
into the spouting Sun.

A world is under
The World, faviform[49] and
tongue-sweet. "Philander" and

"phalange" married in Greek
by "brother." You remember
the Greeks built subcategories
into "love."[50] You were
tangled into "tintinnabulations"[51]
as a child, remembered now

in frotted fingers—lithe
ferox[52] or fierasfer.[53] (How
Night keeps you awake

in dissonant frittiniency.) How
your window makes a
canvas of flavescent sky,

you wish you could
hold on a little
longer (as though holding

somehow makes it yours)
your breath, like clouds,
fringilliform as you swallow
    the Sun back down.

▇▇▇▇▇ LOCUS ISTE

Gauguin and the Pont-Aven School

Briefly ▇▇ amazed. ▇▇ marigold-fields
mell ▇▇▇ and the travellers,
in sudden exile burdened ▇▇
▇▇ gestures, journey to ▇▇

beyond the ▇ severance of ▇▇,
strangeness at doors, ▇ different ▇▇
between the mirror and ▇ window, ▇▇
visible ▇▇ colours of the mind,

▇▇ angels lightning-sketched ▇▇
chalk on the ▇▇ accounts or marigolds
▇ paint runnily embossed, ▇▇ renounced
self-portrait ▇▇ seraph and ▇ storm.

Oranges

The final time; her brilliant frown
like a butterfly on an asphalt ribbon
of electric highway, a last sign

just a warning, a final
appeal. The evaporated rain here
smells of apples and you list

the things that braid
the state of Michigan's vineyards
(like telephone wires deep with birds)

and orchards
(smell like the rain would smell now)
and the asphalt ribbons

and snowflakes that never pack
and gang violence
and the Motor City, great and burning,

you name the lakes that halo
the state of Michigan
you think of all the better things

there are to think about
as you breathe deeply
the menthol glass that eats

your lungs just like it was
formed and the rain that never
    quite

        falls.

Your mother's eyes
when she brought

you oranges in prison
and you cupped them
in your palms, small breasts,

you hoarded them,
the small suns
of these four walls

and four walls
unnumbered fluorescent days
when you hoped for a dark sleep.

The oranges blackened
slowly, press your thumbs
in the wounds,

fester bitter like the oranges
would have been in your mouth.
You breathe sand

and face Mecca,
contemplate your maleness
too often; aberrant,

the hands you've made rough
would have been, should be
while you scream violent

hymns. The rain has stopped
almost falling an, without knowing,
you wasted

all the names, staggered roads
mapped across the palms
of an old man, blind

crumbled stone
that travels through
illness, lean

seasons; the kiss of that
blonde-haired girl whose name
you can't remember, the kiss

of the dark-haired girl
whose name you can't remember,
the kiss of that half-done woman

who was tired of fighting.
Lay across your palm
like a string of beads—counted;

    when you stopped believing
        in the taste of oranges.

Morning comes too soon for Walter Ong[54]

"I am known
this way;" stultified,

Night lifts her
skirt just high

enough to see
that privacy is

a modern invention.
Her hair is

parted with stars,
slips through fingers—

the locks like
moments opening. "I

was a clumsy
child," I whispered

against her split
lip. Tastes like

blood and roadway
roar, "Eloquence seems

almost a selfish
luxury." She breathes
    into me.

Driving Home in the Dark, Cheating the Speed Limit

    I regard this gypsy curse
laid deep on me like this sad season
regarding the disapproval of the traffic lights

    (their lidded and uninterested gazes)
the words that are inherent
in this far-cry city of dark intent

I suppose Frank O'Hara would throw
a fig[55] against the judgment
of that golden eye[56] high above

    this self-same self-made
uninspected place unknowing
what it knows and uncaring

    the night we mixed whiskey sours
with good scotch in discarded bottles
(lacking glasses) how that girl

    slanted her gaze at my lit cigarette
her thick hair and copper
cynicism how her mouth

    unexpectedly tasted sticky
and reminded me of well bourbon
over ice when she sighed

    (don't ask me to leave) this impossible
thing herculean (don't tell me
about what I cannot have)

  apologetic but my resolve before
we said goodbye (Who am I?)
and the walk home drinking

  from the bottle (it was good scotch)
reached furtively from my bag, whoever saw,
regarding lazily this monument built

  to science the building of things over
ruin. I would talk about the moon
but to what end?

For George

that moment
you were Jay Gatsby
in the lightning field
our hands not quite touching
waiting to be scarred too
and your name ran
from my mouth
like water

You can't just go off and be a Ginsberg, no matter when
you are, so I'll get on the bus with Kesey and Cassady just start
believing that we're all four-dimensional beings in three-
dimensional bodies locked in two-dimensional space[57] (the space
of gestures, he says, but that's just the speed talking) someday
1964 will roll around again while we're trying to piss off Kerouac
(because he crystallized too quick) and we'll HOWL over
dictaphone[58] recordings pretending to be Coltrane but we'll
remember O'Hara (always checking twice for Jeeps both ways
before crossing the beach)[59] "Oh the Harpy's claws on
Gertrude Stein," we say over beers in Hoboken or some
godforsaken place where the medical tides come in strongest
at sunset, listen to Houston count down on the radio as though
they're sending Timothy Leary into space[60] every day, wonder
where Bukowski kept the last good piece of Jack's liver
bequeathed to him that winter Sunday ad it's all science:
the way words play together, acoustics in the submarine tube
of the deeper skull. Starkly Famished[61] apart from the rules,
the stations of something faraway, farewell. Whether to stay
here deep in the bus where we aren't who we are, just
pranksters and unchoreographed duets on acid or
cannabinoids. We don't drink too much or just enough because
we're artists who don't know our own equipment. We just want
to be old enough to be Beats or Hippies or beatniks or
no-good-niks, to prattle and picnic and pray to speak concrete
and disenfranchisement to know what goes on under
the deserts deep in cities. I only know the dead language
of not belonging here—

                                  (excerpt from a voicemail)
                                  September (maybe) 2014

Notes:

1. ϕ. The mathematical relationship between distances within figures and forms. Often cited as the innate sense of the "visually beautiful."
2. This poem contains lines quoted from "Bonfire, Jetty" by Robert Fernandez, "A Daughter" by Xochiquetzal Candelaria, and "Black Bird" by Zeeshaw Sahil.
3.
4. This is a reference to John Kennedy Toole's *A Confederacy of Dunces*.
5.
6. This poem takes its title from a review of *Religion and the Decline of Magic* by Keith Thomas as appeared in the Listener written by Ronald Blythe. It is also cited in Tenebrae by Geoffrey Hill.

7.

8.

9. Former from Latin "anxius" (distress); latter from Greek "ekstasis" (standing outside oneself)

10.

11.

12. The Übermensch is Nietzsche's answer to the questions of Nihilism. The tenants of the "superman" and his morality stand in direct contradiction to Kant's morality and the search for truth.

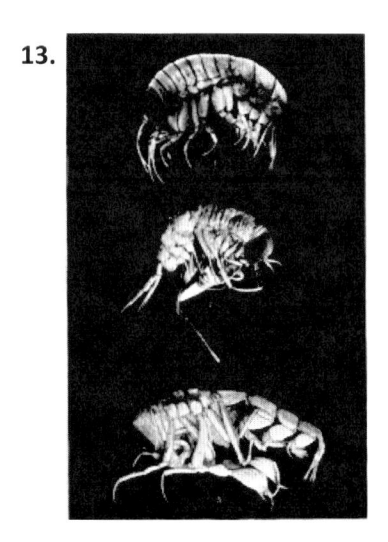

13.

14. From Ecclesiastes Chapter 3.

15.

16. Literally translated "the work of life." A system of Chinese breathing mediations.
17. "And the vessel that he made of clay was marred in the hand of the potter: so he made it again another vessel, as seemed good to the potter to make it." (King James Version)
18. A note about this form: this is an elaboration of sestina in monorhyme scheme. By creating something intentionally difficult, I was hoping to create contrast between meaning and non-meaning that can be read with varying significance.
19. This quote is taken from Simone Weil's *First and Last Notebooks* trans. Richard Rees (page 47).
20. Splitting the tongues of different songbirds is a myth that persists from the Middle Ages. It was believed that if the birds tongue were "freed" it could mimic human speech. This was also something said to be done by witches with the raven "familiars" so that the Devil could speak through them.

21.

22. In ancient Greek, most notably in the myth of Orpheus, magic and music were interchangeable. Music (and the ability to create music) was considered shamanic and more directly in concert with the gods.

23. This refers to an apparition of the Virgin Mary that appeared repeatedly to three shepherd children near the village of Fatima, Portugal (where the visions are still celebrated by pilgrimages today). The children were said to have received prophesies of the future, one of which that wasn't to be revealed in their lifetimes and was given over to the Pope for safe-keeping that still hasn't been acknowledged or revealed by the Vatican.

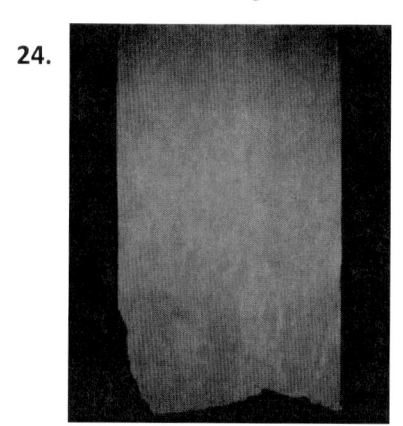

24.

25. Published in 1631, this edition of the Bible was ordered destroyed because, in copying the text, someone forgot the "not" in "Thou shalt not commit adultery." Alternately known as the Adulterous Bible.

26. Three giants from Greek mythology who assisted the Olympians in the overthrow of the Titans after Zeus released them from Tartarus.

27. Egyptian women are thought to have been heavily tattooed in patterns of concentric circles or dots on the thighs and lower abdomen which would expand with the progress of a pregnancy.

28. In Catholic dogma (and more increasingly, popular culture), this is the name for the spear that pierced the side of Christ at the crucifixion.

29.

30. This is a set of sacraments in Catholic faiths giving provision over those who are believed to be dying. It is also known as "Anointing the sick" and is comprised of a series of prayers and rituals (one of which is the final administration of the Eucharist).

31. This is the acronym given to the series of diagnostic manuals titled *The Diagnostic and Statistic Manual of Mental Disorders* (the IV indicates that it is currently in its fourth edition, the most up-to-date version is the DSM-5 with the DSM-IV-TR between the two editions).

32. Lilith is thought by some scholars of the Talmud to be Adam's first wife and is generally considered to be the progenitor of a class of female demons. She is thought to have been created from dust just as Adam was (and therefore equal to, not subordinate of, him) and was cast out and replaced because she refused to comply with the will of her husband. She fled the garden and was cursed by God that each day she was defiant 100 of her demon children would be killed. She is thought, in popular mythology, to be a succubus and killer of infants.

33. These are the Latin words that hung on the cross above the head of Jesus. Roughly translated "Jesus of Nazareth. King of the Jews."

34. I refer to one of three standards of alignment for the adjustment of needle cartridges on an analog turntable. These standards are based on varying opinions of depth and radius from differing schools of acoustic geometry.

35.

36. Skeptical philosopher, art critic, and writer during the Enlightenment. (1713-1784)

37.

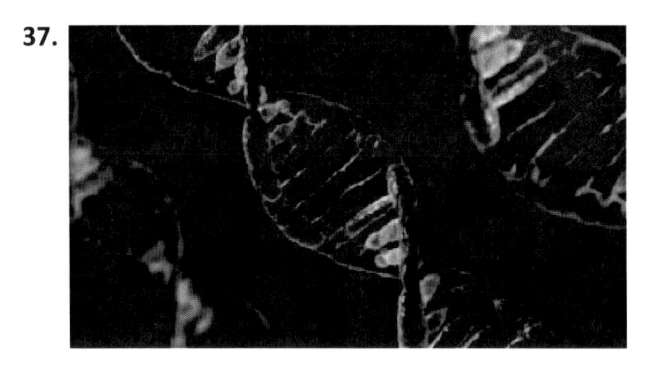

38. The quoted sections in this poem are taken, verbatim, from Simone Weil's *First and Last Notebooks* trans. Richard Rees.

39. In the Middle Ages, lacking blades, monks would use blocks of pumice to scrub the hair from the crowns of their heads. I would imagine that this was incredibly painful and bled a bit before a young monk was used to the practice.

40.

41. Sea god common in many prehistoric cultures. In Homer, he was pursued by Menelaus through the form of many different sea creatures because Proteus' daughter betrayed him.

42. For 2,000 years after the fall of the Roman Empire, the secret recipe behind concrete was lost. Scientists throughout recent history had puzzled over what made Roman buildings so strong. The mixture was rediscovered in 2013 and was found to contain animal blood and volcanic ash in a certain ratio that allowed the concrete to set progressively stronger over time, even under water.

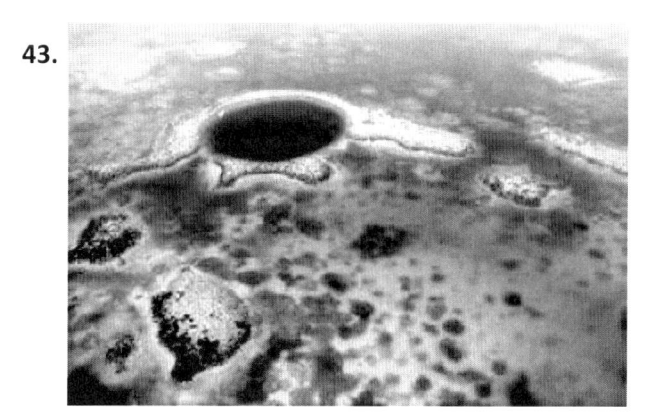

43.

44.

45. This form is adapted from a similar form used by Cliff Weber in *Jack Defeats Ron 100-64*.

46. From a Midwestern colloquialism: "A pole turtle is when you see a turtle on top of a tall pole in the middle of no where and think 'What's that turtle doing there?'" (Referring to something that is glaringly out of place) and from a definition of the word "fustian" which is a roughly woven cloth worn during the 19th century by British workers as symbols of class (the word also refers to overly ornate language in a Shakespearean sense).

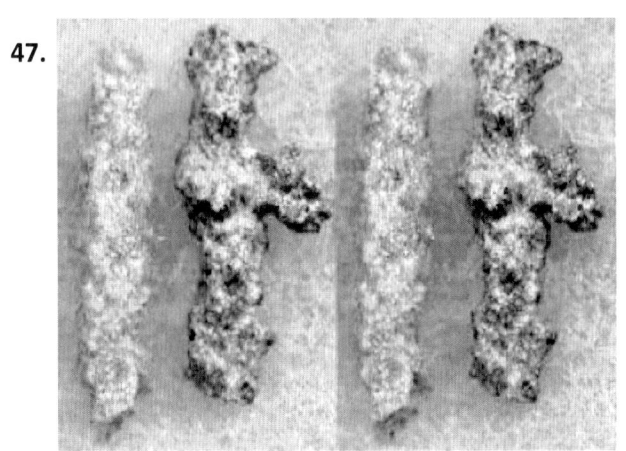

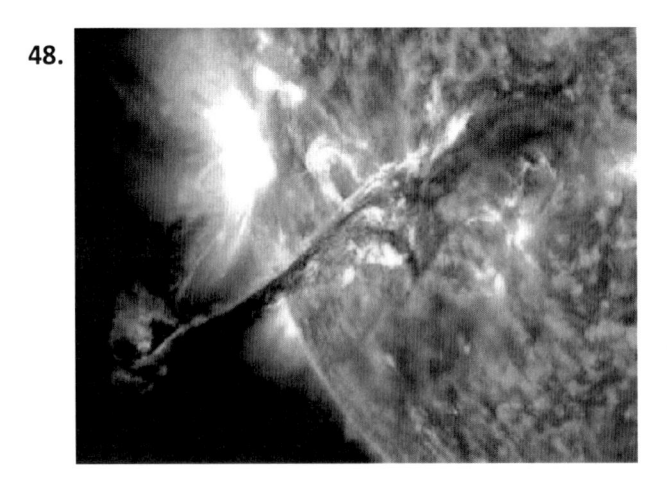

47.

48.

49.

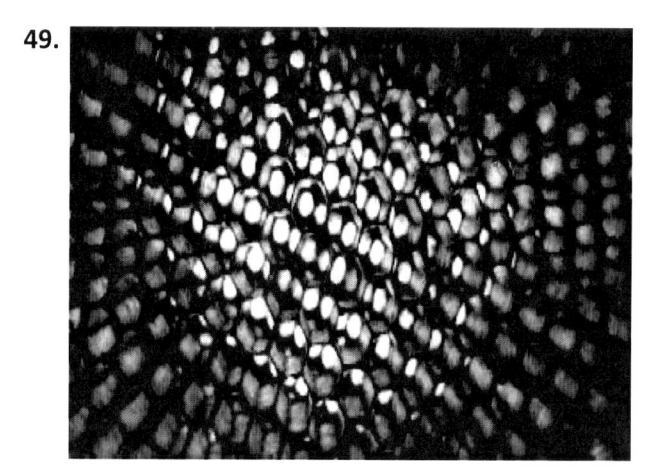

50. The ancient Greeks had six words for love (eros, philia, ludus, agape, pragma, and philautia) all referring to different kinds of love.
51. From Edgar Allan Poe's "The Bells."
52.

53.

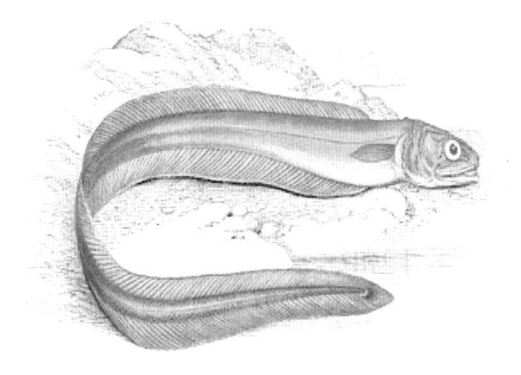

54. Quoted text is taken from an interview with Walter Ong with the exception of "I/was a clumsy/child…"

55.

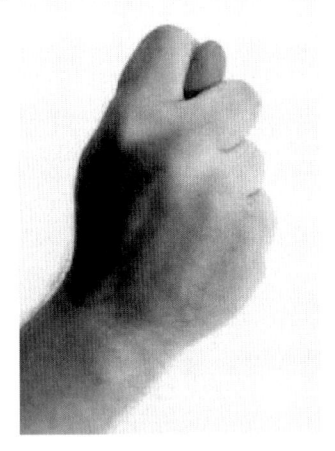

56.

57. Paraphrased from *The Merry Band of Pranksters*, the official movie made by and about the bus tripping pranksters. Neal Cassady was constantly monologuing in the original bus recordings.
58. The Pranksters would sometimes pretend at being jazz musicians, either improving over recordings or simply noodling on old instruments.
59. Alfred Leslie's "The Loading Pier" depicts the death of Frank O'Hara.
60. Timothy Leary had his ashes scattered in space in 1997, though not by NASA but by Celestis, Inc. a private company that has provided 13 space burials to date.
61. This is a combination of two of the nicknames of the Merry Pranksters, Jane "Generally Famished" Burton and Kathy "Stark Naked" Casano.

ABOUT THE AUTHOR

Stephanie Erdman studied at Purdue University and received her master's degree through Indiana University. *Pyrrhonic* is her first full-length publication but her work has appeared in *Eclectica Magazine* and *Twyckenham Notes*. Stephanie lives in Southwest Michigan and works as a professor of English and as a vacuum cleaner technician.